5ᵗʰ Anniversary:

5 Epic Years

Our reflections, memories, thoughts and ideas
for the future.

.

∞

Books With Soul

Somewhere in the desert, sea and forest.

www.bookswithsoul.com

∞

Books with Soul supports copyright for all authors.
Thank you for purchasing a copyrighted edition of this book.
First Edition 2018

ISBN-13: **978-1-949325-10-2**

Life is a collection of moments

-unknown

This journal belongs to a magnificent couple who has shared epic memories:

_____

Inside these pages are their memories, thoughts, inspirations and ideas for the last 5 and the next 5 years.

Date: _____

Given by: _____

Congratulations!

You belong in a very special club. Five years together. Five years of living. Five years is worth celebrating. You are worth celebrating.

This book is for YOUR memories, written in your own words.

Take five minutes a day, a week or even monthly and write a simple thought.
Jot down a memory.
Write a few words.
Write down wishes.
Ideas for the future.
Anything you write will be preserved.
It only takes a minute to record a moment in time forever.

Imagine, you discovered a journal.

A journal written by a friend who passed. Perhaps, it was an aunt, uncle or grandparent whom you never met. Maybe even your mother or father or a sibling who is no longer with you. A person in your life who you miss their words and presence every day.

If they wrote a few words down from time to time, and you were able to read them and reflect back--what a gift that would be. A few words to make you remember, smile and laugh as you read their happy thoughts or favorite color.

Maybe, you have children and you want to remember their first year, or any year, and reflect on their childhood.

Maybe you want your grandchildren to get know their grandparents. Or you have unborn grandchildren, who may never understand what your life was like when they were born. How about great-grandchildren?

Maybe you want to remember your wedding day, your first trip to Europe, or your first home in a new place.

This is a place to scribble a thought a day, or even a memory a week. There are no rules.

This is a book to write a memory or a thought for the future.

Maybe no one will ever read your words--but you. And, in the future you will stumble upon this book made of paper, because it can't be lost when the computer crashes, or when our fast-paced technology changes the way we share or store data. This journal is physical and will always be around.

Maybe one day you will jot down a great quote you heard that day, and it will inspire you or someone you love in the future. Maybe you wrote down a great song, or even a favorite recipe, and your future self will thank you for it.

Maybe it's simply noting the words of your heart, your life together or your secret dreams. A glance back at the best book or movie you read this year. A glance back at your firsts.

Collect your memories.

*Do what you want with this book, there's enough
space for a thought a day, or one a week.
Write some words down for history, to share with others, or
just to enlighten your future self.
Answer a few of the questions and write the date on each
page.*

Share your journey.

*Write your words, together as a couple, or as individuals or
both.*

Hide it, share it or leave it for someone you love.

*Happy 5ᵗʰ year anniversary.
And yes, the Best is Yet to Come.*

www.bookswithsoul.com

"You can't go back and change the beginning, but you can start where you are and change the ending."

-unknown

5 years of
Marriage

60 months of moments together
260 weeks of hugs
1825 days of laughter
43,800 hours full of love and
understanding
2,628,000 minutes of having each other's
back
157,680,000 seconds of you and I

What I most want to remember about
our 5th Anniversary
celebration:

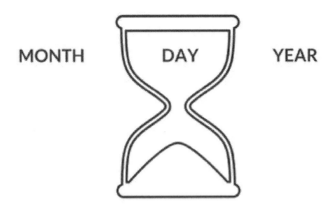

MONTH   DAY   YEAR

If there is one thing I want to remember about this day it is this:

A thought or a sentence for the day:

I want to remember all the places
we have lived:

And we lived here:

Our first vacation we ever took together:

This is the destination we haven't been to yet, but I want to go:

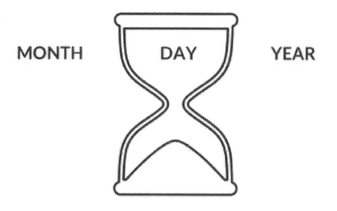

MONTH   DAY   YEAR

If there is one thing I want to remember about this day it is this:

A thought or a sentence for the day:

MONTH 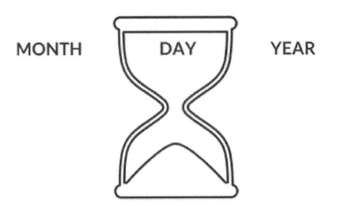 DAY　　　YEAR

Here's a 1st for this year:
The first time I ever....

A thought or a sentence for the
day:

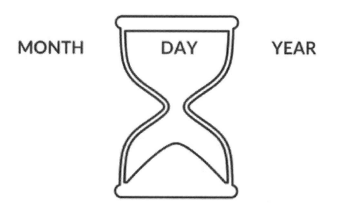

MONTH   DAY   YEAR

**Right now, my favorite song
is:**

**A thought or a sentence for the
day:**

If I had to pick a song that
is our song it is:

We danced to this song at
our wedding:

"To live is the rarest thing in the world. Most people exist, that is all." Oscar Wilde

My favorite quote is:

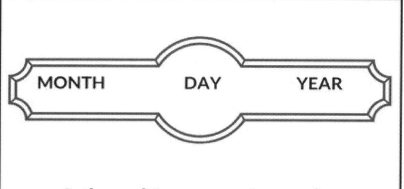

MONTH   DAY   YEAR

A thought or a sentence for the day:

If there is one thing I want to remember about this day it is this:

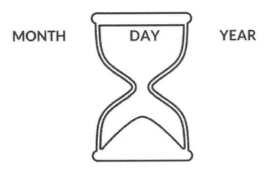

MONTH   DAY   YEAR

This surprised me:

A thought or a sentence for the day:

MONTH 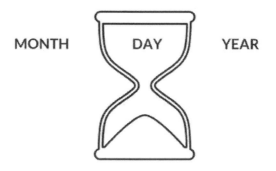 DAY   YEAR

If there is one thing I want to remember about this day it is this:

A thought or a sentence for the day:

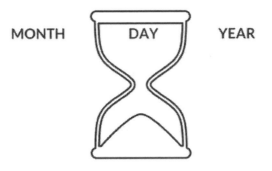

MONTH   DAY   YEAR

At this point in my life, this is my best advice for someone I love:

A thought or a sentence for the day:

The thing that most surprised me about children:

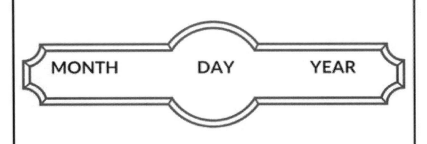

MONTH   DAY   YEAR

A thought or a sentence for the day:

If there is one thing I want to remember about this day it is this:

MONTH 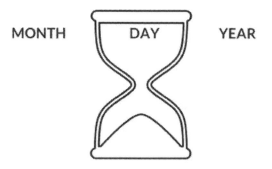 DAY YEAR

A recipe to remember or at least my favorite food of the moment:

A thought or a sentence for the day:

MONTH 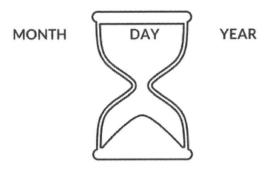 DAY   YEAR

I am most amazed at this new technology:

A thought or a sentence for the day:

"What would you attempt to do if you knew you wouldn't fail?"

— **Anonymous**

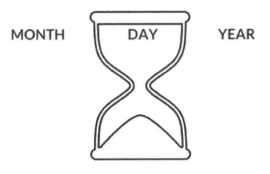

MONTH   DAY   YEAR

This makes me happy:

A thought or a sentence for the day:

Live in the sunshine, swim in the sea, drink the wild air-
Ralph Waldon Emerson

A favorite seaside memory is:

> "Two roads diverged in a wood and I – I took the one less traveled by." – Robert Frost

The most off-the-beaten-path adventure we had:

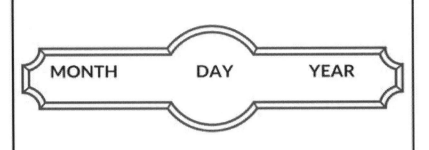

MONTH   DAY   YEAR

A thought or a sentence for the day:

If there is one thing I want to remember about this day it is this:

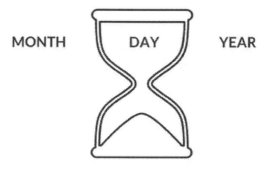

MONTH   DAY   YEAR

If there is one thing I want to remember about this day it is this:

A thought or a sentence for the day:

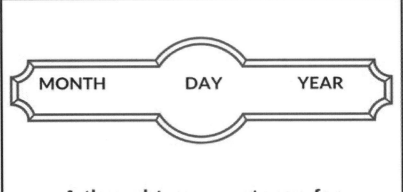

A thought or a sentence for the day:

If there is one thing I want to remember about this day it is this:

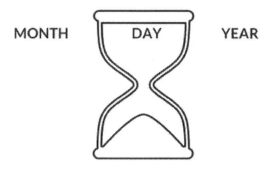

MONTH   DAY   YEAR

Sometimes this makes me anxious:

A thought or a sentence for the day:

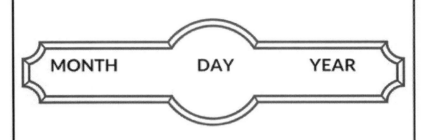

MONTH   DAY   YEAR

A thought or a sentence for the day:

If there is one thing I want to remember about this day it is this:

My favorite animal is:

(A list of the pets we had in 5 years)

Why does time seem to speed up with
each passing year?
This day feels like yesterday:

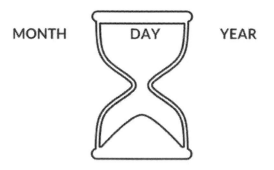

MONTH   DAY   YEAR

**The best book I've read this
year or any year:**

**A thought or a sentence for the
day:**

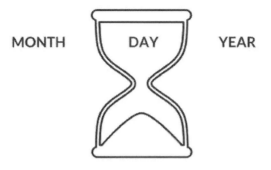

MONTH   DAY   YEAR

If there is one thing I want to remember about this day it is this:

A thought or a sentence for the day:

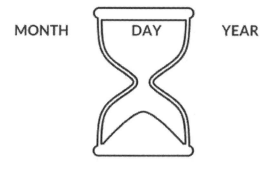

MONTH   DAY   YEAR

I am most shocked by this:

A thought or a sentence for the day:

MONTH 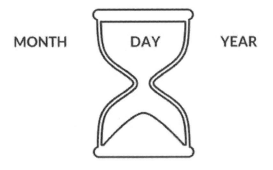 DAY YEAR

If there is one thing I want to remember about this day it is this:

A thought or a sentence for the day:

MONTH 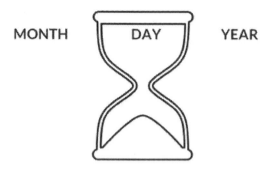 YEAR

I worry most about this:

A thought or a sentence for the day:

MONTH 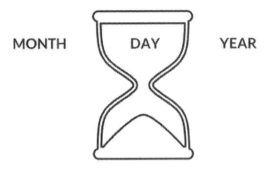 DAY YEAR

If there is one thing I want to remember about this day it is this:

A thought or a sentence for the day:

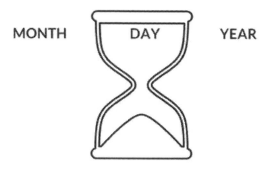

MONTH   DAY   YEAR

My favorite memory from my childhood:

A thought or a sentence for the day:

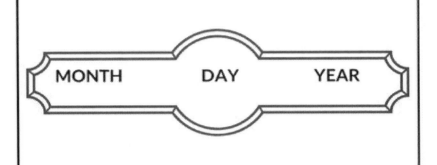

MONTH   DAY   YEAR

A thought or a sentence for the day:

If there is one thing I want to remember about this day it is this:

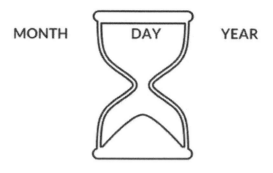

MONTH   DAY   YEAR

I love this old song:

A thought or a sentence for the day:

Die with memories not dreams -unknown

MONTH 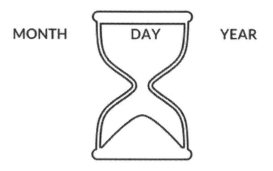 YEAR

If I had to pick my last meal:

A thought or a sentence for the day:

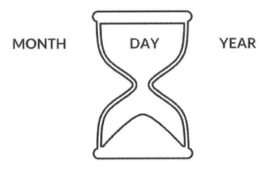

MONTH DAY YEAR

If there is one thing I want to remember about this day it is this:

A thought or a sentence for the day:

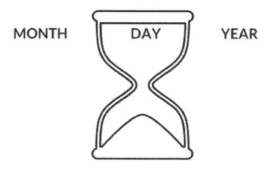

MONTH DAY YEAR

If I could change one thing this year it would be:

A thought or a sentence for the day:

Sometimes we just need to say "Yes" more
often...
This year I'm going to say yes to this:

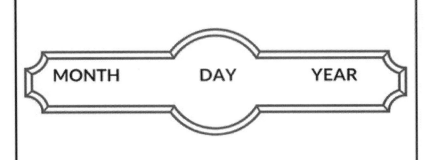

MONTH   DAY   YEAR

A thought or a sentence for the day:

If there is one thing I want to remember about this day it is this:

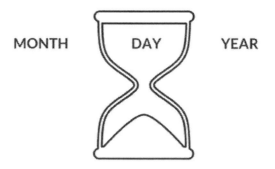

MONTH   DAY   YEAR

If there is one thing I want to remember about this day it is this:

A thought or a sentence for the day:

A great journey I will never forget:

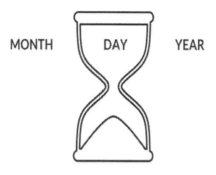

MONTH   DAY   YEAR

If there is one thing I want to remember about this day it is this:

A thought or a sentence for the day:

This year I have been busy with this:

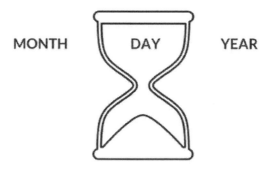

MONTH DAY YEAR

If there is one thing I want to remember about this day it is this:

A thought or a sentence for the day:

Fill your life with adventures not things. Have stories to tell not to stuff to show.

A story of the moment I don't want to forget:

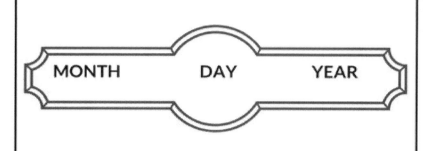

MONTH   DAY   YEAR

A thought or a sentence for the day:

If there is one thing I want to remember about this day it is this:

MONTH 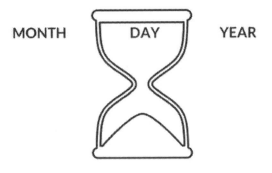 DAY YEAR

**When I think of my favorite
memory of my mother or father
it is this:**

**A thought or a sentence for the
day:**

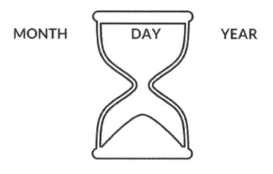

MONTH DAY YEAR

This surprised me:

A thought or a sentence for the day:

MONTH 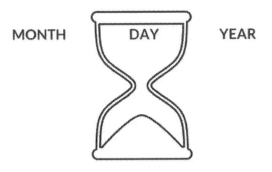 DAY YEAR

The most surprising event that happened this year in the world:

A thought or a sentence for the day:

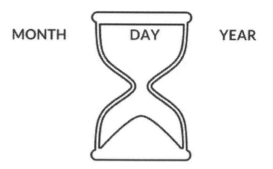

MONTH   DAY   YEAR

I never thought I would see the day:

A thought or a sentence for the day:

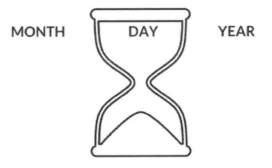

MONTH DAY YEAR

When I think of my biggest accomplishment this year:

A thought or a sentence for the day:

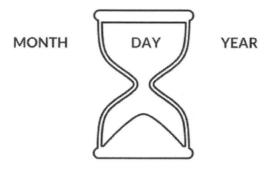

MONTH   DAY   YEAR

If there is one thing I want to remember about this day it is this:

A thought or a sentence for the day:

"Life is either a daring adventure or nothing." -- Helen Keller

One of my favorite adventures this year:

MONTH 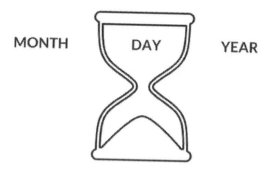 YEAR

If there is one thing I want to remember about this day it is this:

A thought or a sentence for the day:

MONTH 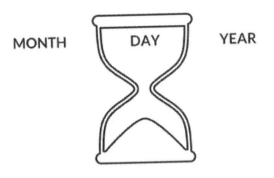 YEAR

Things that make me wonder:

A thought or a sentence for the day:

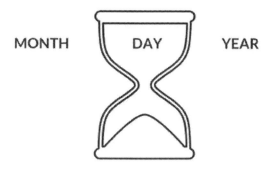

MONTH   DAY   YEAR

If there is one thing I want to remember about this day it is this:

A thought or a sentence for the day:

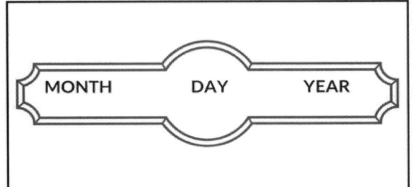

MONTH DAY YEAR

A thought or a sentence for the day:

If there is one thing I want to remember about this day it is this:

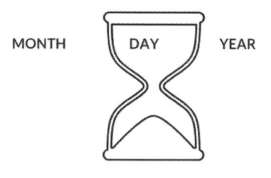

MONTH   DAY   YEAR

I loved this movie:

A thought or a sentence for the day:

This was a funny moment of our 5 years:

We didn't realize this would go on for five years, my aren't we surprised.

One of my favorite memories from meeting you:

The first day
we met:

MONTH 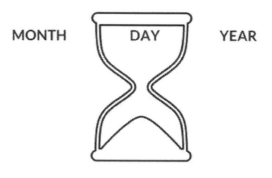 YEAR

I can't believe:

A thought or a sentence for the day:

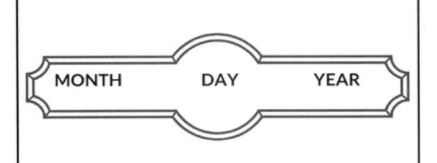

MONTH   DAY   YEAR

A thought or a sentence for the day:

If there is one thing I want to remember about this day it is this:

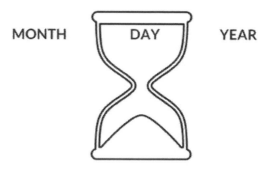

MONTH   DAY   YEAR

I will remember this year for:

A thought or a sentence for the day:

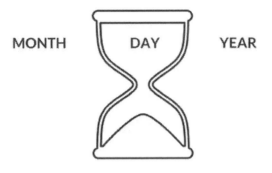

MONTH DAY YEAR

If there is one thing I want to remember about this day it is this:

A thought or a sentence for the day:

MONTH 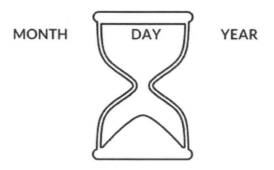 YEAR

**At this point in my life, this is my
best advice for someone I love:**

**A thought or a sentence for the
day:**

The world is big, and I want to get a good look at it before it
gets dark. - John Muir

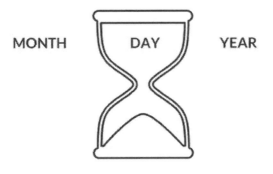

MONTH   DAY   YEAR

If there is one thing I want to remember about this day it is this:

A thought or a sentence for the day:

MONTH 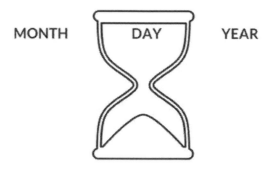 YEAR

I never want to forget:

A thought or a sentence for the day:

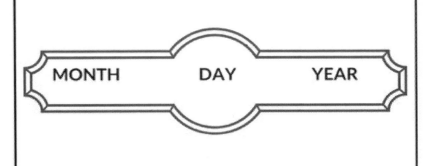

MONTH   DAY   YEAR

A thought or a sentence for the day:

If there is one thing I want to remember about this day it is this:

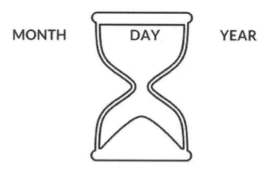

MONTH · DAY · YEAR

The food I can't stand:

A thought or a sentence for the day:

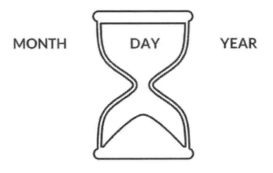

MONTH   DAY   YEAR

If there is one thing I want to remember about this day it is this:

A thought or a sentence for the day:

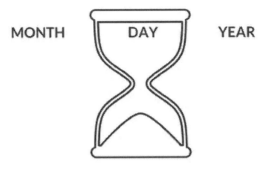

MONTH　　　DAY　　　YEAR

I love this season best of all:

A thought or a sentence for the day:

MONTH 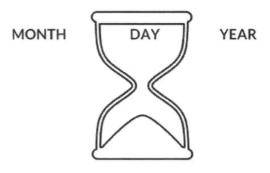 YEAR

This surprised me:

A thought or a sentence for the day:

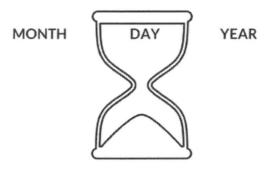

MONTH DAY YEAR

My favorite memory from my childhood:

A thought or a sentence for the day:

MONTH 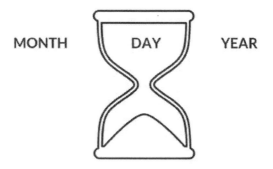 YEAR

If there is one thing I want to remember about this day it is this:

A thought or a sentence for the day:

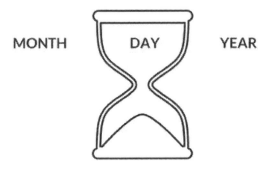

MONTH   DAY   YEAR

If there is one thing I want to remember about this day it is this:

A thought or a sentence for the day:

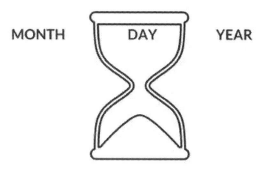

MONTH DAY YEAR

I never want to forget:

A thought or a sentence for the day:

MONTH 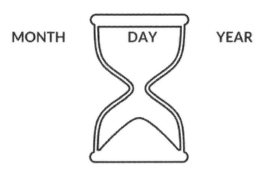 YEAR

I wish I could:

A thought or a sentence for the day:

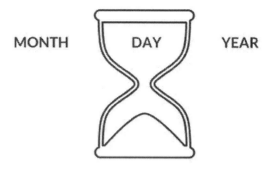

MONTH   DAY   YEAR

If there is one thing I want to remember about this day it is this:

A thought or a sentence for the day:

If I won an all-expense-paid vacation, I would go to:

MONTH 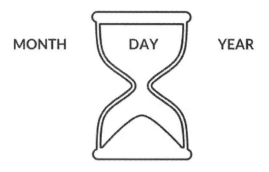 DAY YEAR

If there is one thing I want to remember about this day it is this:

A thought or a sentence for the day:

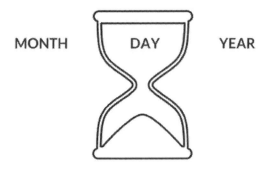

MONTH   DAY   YEAR

If there is one thing I want to remember about this day it is this:

A thought or a sentence for the day:

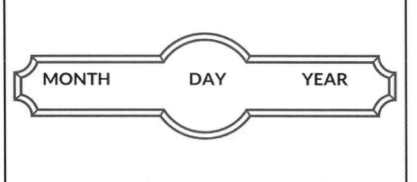

| MONTH | DAY | YEAR |

A thought or a sentence for the day:

If there is one thing I want to remember about this day it is this:

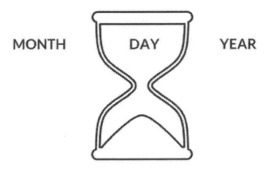

MONTH   DAY   YEAR

If there is one thing I want to remember about this day it is this:

A thought or a sentence for the day:

MONTH 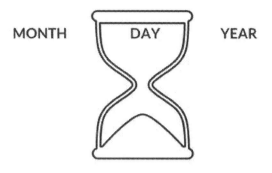 YEAR

I never want to forget:

A thought or a sentence for the day:

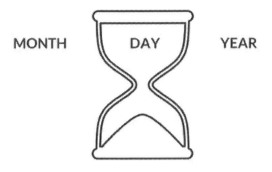

MONTH   DAY   YEAR

If there is one thing I want to remember about this day it is this:

A thought or a sentence for the day:

MONTH 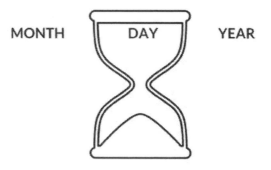 DAY YEAR

My pet peeve of the moment:

**A thought or a sentence for the
day:**

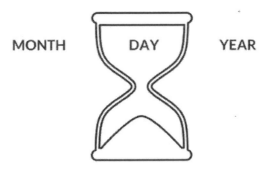

MONTH   DAY   YEAR

If there is one thing I want to remember about this day it is this:

A thought or a sentence for the day:

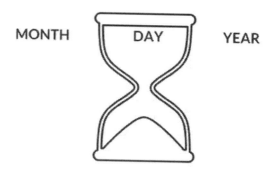

MONTH DAY YEAR

I love this old song:

A thought or a sentence for the day:

I love this new song:

One of the best Vacations Ever:

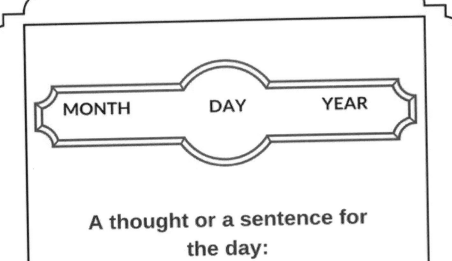

MONTH   DAY   YEAR

A thought or a sentence for the day:

If there is one thing I want to remember about this day it is this:

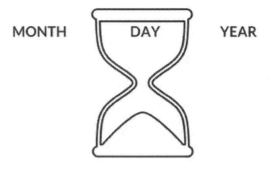

MONTH   DAY   YEAR

Right now my favorite vacation was:

A thought or a sentence for the day:

MONTH 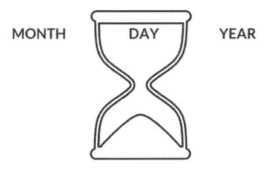 DAY YEAR

When I think of my favorite memory of my mother or father it is this:

A thought or a sentence for the day:

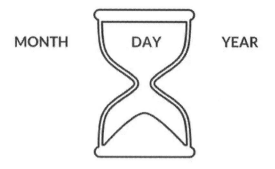

MONTH   DAY   YEAR

If there is one thing I want to remember about this day it is this:

A thought or a sentence for the day:

MONTH 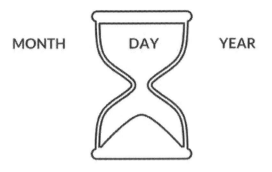 DAY　　　YEAR

If there is one thing I want to remember about this day it is this:

A thought or a sentence for the day:

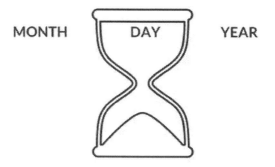

MONTH   DAY   YEAR

At this point in my life, this is my best advice for someone I love:

A thought or a sentence for the day:

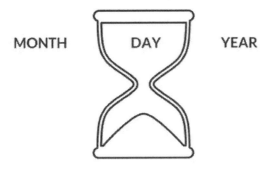

MONTH   DAY   YEAR

If there is one thing I want to remember about this day it is this:

A thought or a sentence for the day:

MONTH 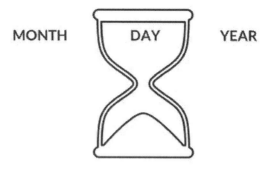 DAY YEAR

Things that make me wonder:

A thought or a sentence for the day:

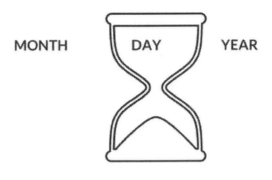

MONTH DAY YEAR

I loved this movie:

A thought or a sentence for the day:

MONTH 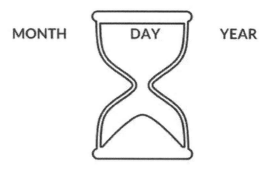 YEAR

I never want to forget:

A thought or a sentence for the day:

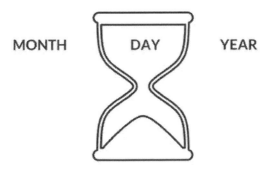

MONTH   DAY   YEAR

If there is one thing I want to remember about this day it is this:

A thought or a sentence for the day:

I need more of this:

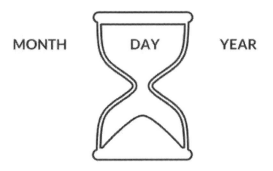

MONTH   DAY   YEAR

If there is one thing I want to remember about this day it is this:

A thought or a sentence for the day:

I dream of this place:

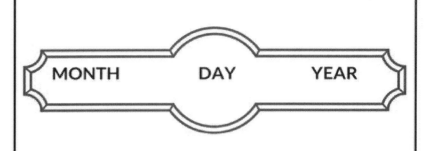

MONTH   DAY   YEAR

A thought or a sentence for the day:

If there is one thing I want to remember about this day it is this:

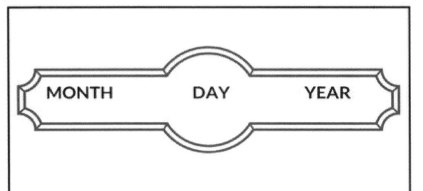

MONTH   DAY   YEAR

A thought or a sentence for the day:

If there is one thing I want to remember about this day it is this:

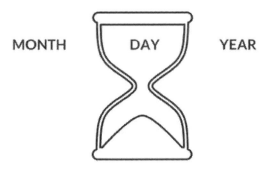

MONTH　　　DAY　　　YEAR

If there is one thing I want to remember about this day it is this:

A thought or a sentence for the day:

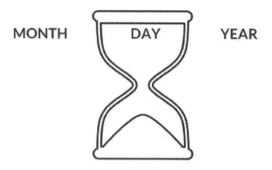

MONTH DAY YEAR

I will remember this year for:

A thought or a sentence for the day:

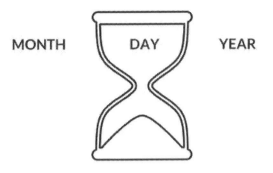

MONTH   DAY   YEAR

If there is one thing I want to remember about this day it is this:

A thought or a sentence for the day:

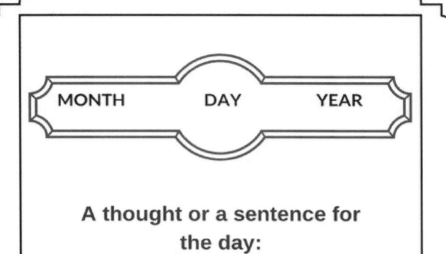

MONTH   DAY   YEAR

A thought or a sentence for the day:

If there is one thing I want to remember about this day it is this:

MONTH 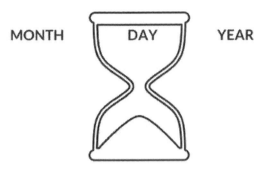 YEAR

I can't believe:

A thought or a sentence for the day:

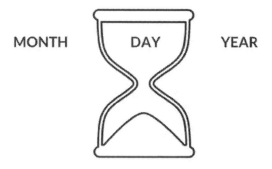

MONTH   DAY   YEAR

If there is one thing I want to remember about this day it is this:

A thought or a sentence for the day:

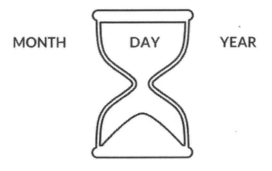

MONTH   DAY   YEAR

If there is one thing I want to remember about this day it is this:

A thought or a sentence for the day:

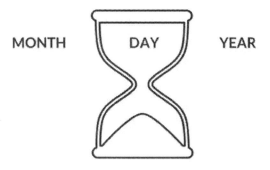

MONTH DAY YEAR

If there is one thing I want to remember about this day it is this:

A thought or a sentence for the day:

MONTH 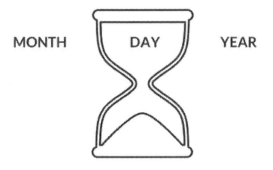 DAY   YEAR

If there is one thing I want to remember about this day it is this:

A thought or a sentence for the day:

MONTH 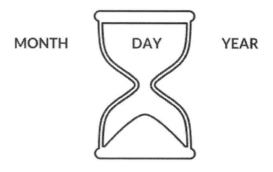 YEAR

If there is one thing I want to remember about this day it is this:

A thought or a sentence for the day:

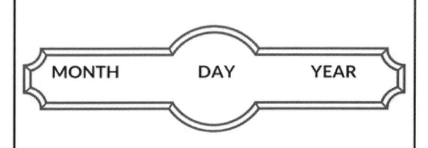

MONTH   DAY   YEAR

A thought or a sentence for the day:

If there is one thing I want to remember about this day it is this:

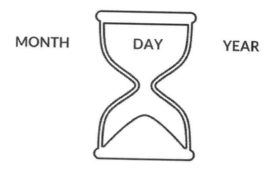

MONTH DAY YEAR

If there is one thing I want to remember about this day it is this:

A thought or a sentence for the day:

Always take the scenic route
makes me think of:

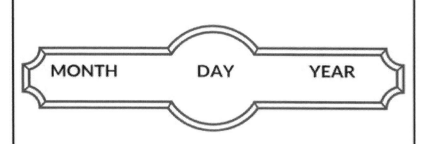

MONTH   DAY   YEAR

A thought or a sentence for the day:

If there is one thing I want to remember about this day it is this:

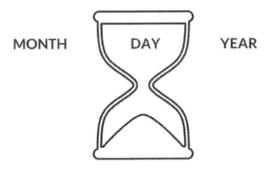

MONTH   DAY   YEAR

If there is one thing I want to remember about this day it is this:

A thought or a sentence for the day:

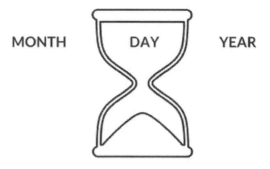

MONTH   DAY   YEAR

If there is one thing I want to remember about this day it is this:

A thought or a sentence for the day:

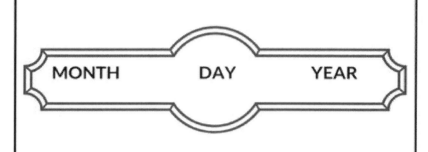

| MONTH | DAY | YEAR |

A thought or a sentence for the day:

If there is one thing I want to remember about this day it is this:

A lesson I learned as a child:

A few of my favorite things:

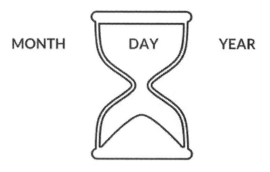

MONTH   DAY   YEAR

If there is one thing I want to remember about this day it is this:

A thought or a sentence for the day:

We really wanted to name our kids:

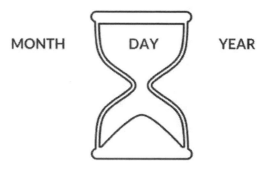

MONTH   DAY   YEAR

If there is one thing I want to remember about this day it is this:

A thought or a sentence for the day:

MONTH 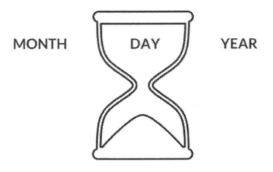 DAY YEAR

If there is one thing I want to remember about this day it is this:

A thought or a sentence for the day:

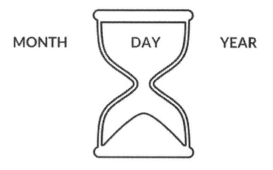

MONTH   DAY   YEAR

If there is one thing I want to remember about this day it is this:

A thought or a sentence for the day:

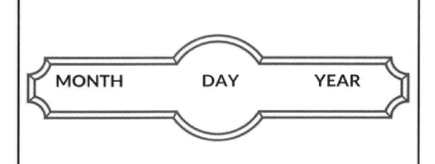

MONTH   DAY   YEAR

A thought or a sentence for the day:

If there is one thing I want to remember about this day it is this:

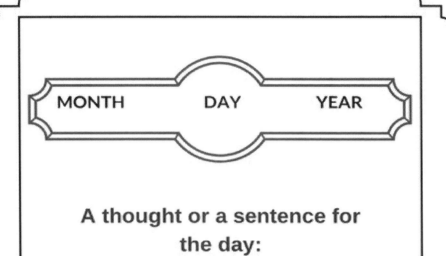

MONTH   DAY   YEAR

A thought or a sentence for the day:

If there is one thing I want to remember about this day it is this:

Top five movies we love:

Top five foods from the past we crave:

Top five bands we love:

Top five TV shows we love:

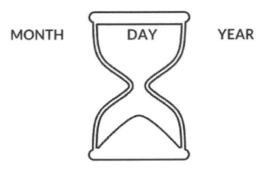

MONTH   DAY   YEAR

I will remember this year for:

A thought or a sentence for the day:

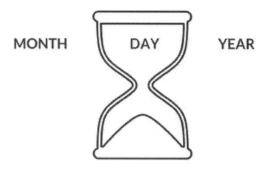

MONTH DAY YEAR

If there is one thing I want to remember about this day it is this:

A thought or a sentence for the day:

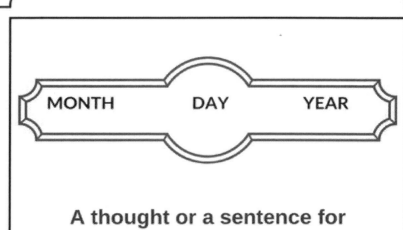

MONTH   DAY   YEAR

A thought or a sentence for the day:

If there is one thing I want to remember about this day it is this:

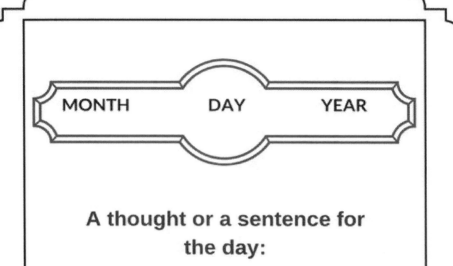

MONTH   **DAY**   **YEAR**

A thought or a sentence for the day:

If there is one thing I want to remember about this day it is this:

Love is not about how many days, months, or years, you have been together. Love is about how much you love each other every single day.

-unknown

My favorite thing about being married is:

When we get to the end of our lives together, the house we had, the cars we drove, the things we possessed won't matter. What will matter is that I had you, and you had me.
-unknown

I love this about you:

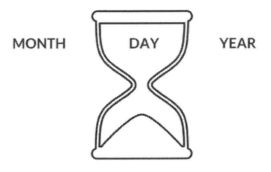

MONTH   DAY   YEAR

If there is one thing I want to remember about this day it is this:

A thought or a sentence for the day:

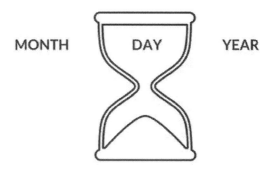

MONTH DAY YEAR

If there is one thing I want to remember about this day it is this:

A thought or a sentence for the day:

Love is patient, love is kind. Love does not envy, it does not boast, it is not proud. It does not dishonor others, it is not self-seeking, it is not easily angered, it keeps no record of wrongs. Love does not delight in evil but rejoices with the truth. It always protects, always trusts, always hopes, always perseveres....1 Corinthians 13

I hope I never forget:

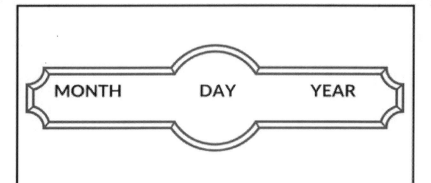

MONTH   DAY   YEAR

A thought or a sentence for the day:

If there is one thing I want to remember about this day it is this:

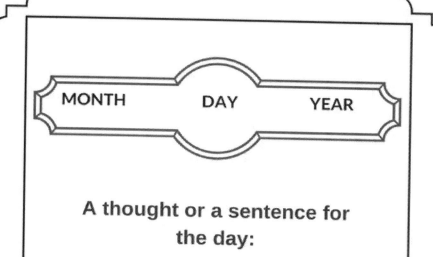

MONTH   DAY   YEAR

A thought or a sentence for the day:

If there is one thing I want to remember about this day it is this:

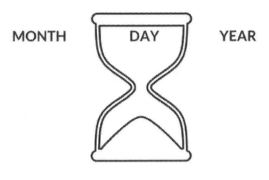

MONTH   DAY   YEAR

I can't believe:

A thought or a sentence for the day:

MONTH 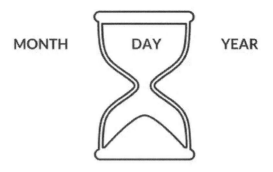 DAY YEAR

If there is one thing I want to remember about this day it is this:

A thought or a sentence for the day:

MONTH 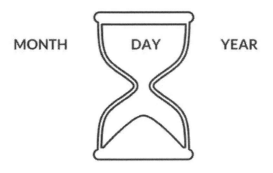 DAY   YEAR

If there is one thing I want to remember about this day it is this:

A thought or a sentence for the day:

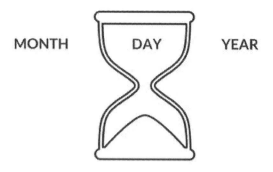

MONTH DAY YEAR

If there is one thing I want to remember about this day it is this:

A thought or a sentence for the day:

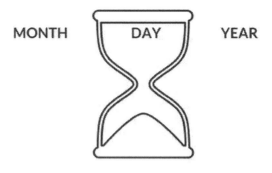

MONTH | DAY | YEAR

I never want to forget:

A thought or a sentence for the day:

Remember

When?

Anniversary editions available on Amazon:
1st Anniversary: One Epic Year
5th Anniversary: Five Epic Years
10th Anniversary: Ten Epic Years
15th Anniversary: Fifteen Epic Years
20th Anniversary: Twenty Epic Years
25th Anniversary: Twenty-five Epic Years
30th Anniversary: Thirty Epic Years
35th Anniversary: Thirty-five Epic Years
40th Anniversary: Forty Epic Years
45th Anniversary: Forty-five Epic Years
50th Anniversary: Fifty Epic Years

Perfect Anniversary Gift

Books With Soul

Books with Soul believes in sharing gifts that inspire and motivate
others to create memories and keep a record of the story of their life.
What if… you had a record of your memories or someone you loved?

INSPIRATION COMES IN ALL SIZES, SHAPES AND IDEAS

WE believe every life is worth a few written words to pass on or reflect on in the
future.
You don't have to be an author to tell the story of your life. Just be you.
Today will someday be the good old days, remember them.
Books with Soul offers inspirational journals with questions and thoughts to help
record memories for the most novice of journalers, great birthday, milestone,
wedding and baby gifts. Help someone write their life story.

Questions? Email info@bookswithsoul.com
We appreciate every reader, every traveler and recorder of history.
We would love if you took the time to write a
review on Amazon and let us know if the books motivated you.

Find more journals, inspiration, diaries, coloring books and gifts for every
milestone at:
www.bookswithsoul.com

If you would like to have a personalized journal for
an organization, company,
group, club,
or activity, contact
Books with Soul.
Special unique journals in 25 quantities or more can
be created.

*if someone bought you this journal, pay it forward and buy a journal
for someone
you care about.
Help them write the story of their life.

Books with Soul ™

was inspired from a lover of music and life, who believed in the soul. He had a collection of wonderful things. Physical memories you could read, touch, and listen to- including thousands of vinyl albums. Old school music, that lasts forever. In 2018, he passed away from brain cancer, but his memory lives on as others go old school. Collect pieces of your history, put pencil to paper, and record written memories. A physical book will not be lost in the cloud, and will last longer than a lifetime.

Keep a record of the story of your life. Your Words. Your Pages.

This is for you Mark.

Bookswith**soul**.com
Your Words. Your Pages.